Happy
Fathers Day!

Rick B.

Savvy

Jim Are

Savvy...

A Golden Dog's View
of This Human World

By Savannah Adams
(with a little help from her owner)

ISBN 978-0-692-01208-6

Have you ever wondered what dogs actually think and feel of the human world they inhabit?

Painting of Savvy created by Personal Creations

Here is a "pen in paw" first hand look at golden retriever columnist Savannah "Savvy" Adams' four year writings on her canine world co-existing with everything she encounters!

Savvy started "writing" columns in 2007 for The Lakes News Shopper, a free circulation newspaper in Dickinson County, northwest Iowa. "My Point of View" by Savannah Adams was an instant hit! From reader feedback and comments, to various dogs and cats writing her letters to the editor, to public receptions like parades and charity events; Savvy became known to thousands!

After many reader comments such as "Why doesn't Savvy write a book?" or "Her stuff beats your editorials 10 to 1", Savvy and I had a long discussion on the merits and work involved in a potential book deal. With the bribe of extra chew bones and more pheasant hunting time, she went barkingly bonkers over the thought she could actually pull it off.

"We" agreed to divide her columns into the general parts you will find in this book. **They are:**

One - "Savvy", How I Got Here

Two - What I Really Think!

Three - My Canine and Other Friends (and Enemies)

Four - Stuff I forgot in the First Three Parts!

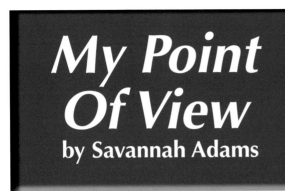

My Point Of View
by Savannah Adams

Part One

🐾

How I Got Here!

1

"Dog Days" of Summer '07

Hello out there to all canines and their owner/friends who read them my column when I take pen in paw. As many of you regular readers know (and for the benefit of summer "man's best friend" owners), I'm a 17 month old Golden Retriever who came to live on the north shore of Lake Minnewashta in April '06 with John & Mary Adams.

To me, everyday of summer is a "dog day," meaning it's grrrreat to be around the Lakes area cause there's so much to do! I'd like to tell you in this report some of my favorite canine cavorts.

• I love the bike trail! We have the neatest part of the trail that my owner and I cover three times a day. We get out of his van by the Henderson Woods start on Minnewashta, walk through down to the bridge, and if I've been real good on the walk, we go over the bridge and scoot on down by Lower Gar Lake almost all the way to the beginning of a park. Talk about neat stuff to see! Turtles–I've only played with painteds, he told me I must stay away from a snapper (whatever that is?) if I ever see one. Rabbits–I try to chase them but I get reined in pretty quickly (he's funny that way). Squirrels–I just detest those animals. They always run away from me and go up a tree. How fair is that? Pheasants–this is where my owner tells me he knew I would be a hunting dog, cause I smelled some off the trail, and flushed them up. And dogs–I've met so many friends, Zena, Echo, Jazz, Sunshine, Cisco, and a new friend, Coby, a cute cocker spaniel pup half my age! (Of course, my best friend is still my neighborhood buddy Lucy). But these new friends are cool!

• The boat – what a toot! I love to ride up front where I can see all the boats going by. I've even barked greetings to a few other lucky dogs like me who get to be on the water. I think going under that bridge by West & East Okoboji is fun, there's always lot of things to view and check out. Funny thing about the water…I was roaring around on the dock and I fell in. Now no one had taught me how to swim, I just did, and it was so much fun.

And there's so much more going on all the time, I don't get bored! Course, I sleep a lot too. And writing these columns is fun, cause I usually get letters from dogs on how their lives are; in fact, last time our neighbor's cat Raider wrote me a feline view of canines…let's say he and I "tolerate and respect" each other. And I made a new friend already before this column came out – I got a neat letter from Zoe, a golden retriever pup from Ruthven! It's in this paper!

So, have a grrrreat 4th of July week!!

Barkingly yours…

Savvy

Of Animals...And People

It's time to take pen in paw and visit with you again! According to my owner, judging by the comments he gets when I write an editorial compared to his, I should be writing every week, and he can write every other month! As I barked this summer..."It's a dog's life," and that means it's a good life!

I've been coming across a lot of animals and people lately. Now, the people have been grrreat...the canine consensus is still out on the animals!

The animals around here keep me on my paws. Whenever we go for trail walks it seems like I meet new ones. About a month ago we went down when it was dark. We had a lantern, and I had my training collar on. As we came into the woods, I saw this gray and white creature with an ugly tail, and I wanted to go after it. But my owner kept me with him cause he said it was a coyote. I wasn't afraid...but it was weird. I'm trying to learn to stay away from raccoons cause I guess they don't like dogs!

The ones that drive me Barkingly Bonkers are squirrels. My owner calls them rodents. I can tell you, as one canine to another, whenever you chase them and they run up a tree, they yell at you...I know their language, and what they're saying is definitely not repeatable, at least for family dogs! I did catch one...and I won't go into all the details, but all you need to know is that there is one less rodent around to bug me!

I'm getting my best friend Lucy (the chocolate lab who lives across the street at the Walkers) back in normal playing behavior. She had an accident with a car last month, and I've missed her a lot! But now we check out our front door nightly and bark to meet each other and roar around!

I've met some more dog lovers, and are they doggone wonderful. My owner takes me up to Spirit Lake to visit Dale & Sarah Lundstrom. I guess they owned golden retriever kennels when his children were growing up (you know, the ones with the neat grandkids I play with. I like the parents, but I love those grandkids!) Anyway, whenever they have coffee, Sarah gives me cookies if I'm good, and when cookies are involved, I try to be really good! I guess some great dogs lived in those kennels, and several pups went to our home to live years ago.

That's it from Oak St. You canines and canine owners, drop me a line if you have time.

Falling...for you,

Savvy

"Dogging It" During The Holidays With My Friends...

Merry Christmas to all you canines and canine owners out there! As a golden retriever, I don't really understand what Merry Christmas means, but I've heard it a lot, and I think I learned about it this weekend!

Saturday my owner and I went to Spirit Lake to visit two really neat friends of his, Dale and Sarah Lundstrom. I always love going there cause Sarah bakes treats for me. This time it was muffins, and I ate three of them! They always spend a lot of time visiting about the "old days" (that was before me).

As I wrote you before, Dale and Sarah owned the Lundstrom Kennels, from where many, many, many, many golden retriever pups and their parents lived. A few became national and regional hunting and field trial champs. (I don't know what a field trial is, but I think it's like hunting with my owner. Anyway, we go after pheasants in a field, it becomes a trial to get one, the way he shoots…) And many puppies went to good homes and became loving family members (like me).

Dog-gone it, I've been barking on here…but this "tail" has a happy ending. The Lundstrom goldens went all over the plains, fields, and waterways. I only know my mom and dad, and they didn't come from the kennels. But two things back some 30-40 years ago, some of the Lundstrom hunters had - I have! A black diamond on my tongue and a brown nose! They talked with my owner about my "pedigree". I think that means when pets agree on something! Anyway, even if I can't prove I'm related to them, I'm going to claim them as my great, great, great owners too!

As we left, my owner and they exchanged presents while I went outside to check out one more time the empty kennels…I could sure smell and sense there had been some great dogs living there "in the old days." I didn't have a canine clue what the presents were for, so I barked at him, and he told me while driving home that that is why you give Christmas presents to your friends, cause long ago a special present was given to the world…(that must have been before hunting dogs!)

Anyway, as soon as I got home, I ran across the street to tell my best friend Lucy about Christmas and giving a present to your friends. We both howled with glee, and growled over the details of what we would give. Lucy told me she'd give me an extra romp around the yard everyday…and I told her I'd bring her one of my doggy chew bones. What a great idea Christmas is!

Now that I'm older (2 years old on Dec. 5, chewing a lot less, and enjoying pheasant hunting even more) I'm starting to understand more things…I hope all of you will remember your friends.

Have a howling happy holiday season…

 **Savvy**

Me At Work!

Many of you readers want to know how I write my columns in the Lakes News. So as you can see, here I am at my desk writing this week's doggie diatribe!

Actually, the picture you see is a painting of me, given to my owner by his daughter Julie (who had taken my picture to an artist). She, by the way, brought me into his life some four years ago! It was after his last Golden Retriever, Blaze, had passed away that Julie bought me, a young puppy from a kennel east of Des Moines.

I had no way of knowing how much fun I was going to have coming to Lake Minnewashta; and also how I might be related to a wonderful Golden Retriever kennel that was in Spirit Lake! It was on one of my first visits with my owner to his friends Dale and Sarah Lundstrom that we started thinking that my love of pheasant hunting and retrieving might be "doggedly descended" from their field trial and hunting dogs of years before I was around.

As you can see from the picture above, I have two features of their dogs, a brown nose (not black) and a little bump on my head. And down on the bottom of this letter you see another marking, a black diamond on my tongue. I am a Lundstrom Golden!

We had a great time this weekend! Our Des Moines family all came up for Easter. Scout, the Golden Retriever, and Cyrus, the Bulldog, brought along their families.

We three dogs took our families for long hikes through CRP land my owner and I hunt on in the fall. "We" found badger holes,

"smelled" pheasants, came across some deer bones, found a poor rabbit that had the misfortune to meet a coyote, and many other "scenting tales!"

That's about it from Oak Street. I'll take pen in paw soon!

Hope there's spring in your step!

Savvy

6

My Easter Weekend Visitors

Hello again to all canines and canine owners! This past weekend I had a special visitor to share my utility room here on Lake Minnewashta. Maggie, a 13-year-old Beagle came up from Des Moines with the family she owns, Heather, Brad, Eli, Olivia and Isaac. We also had Julie and Mya here, but they left their two Bulldogs, Cyrus and Lola, at home.

Maggie and I had good conversations each night we slept in my "room." She never

Maggie

used to like me too much; 'cause I was a puppy and I always wanted to play. She had played a lot in her first 12 years, but now she just likes to "cool it" and relax, so I don't bug her as much anymore, and we get along fine!

Maggie was a real good friend of Blaze, the golden retriever who lived with my owner for 15 years. She told me all about Blaze, how much fun they had together when Maggie visited, all the walks they took together, and how they both loved to sniff out rabbits or other fun animals to chase after. So I got to learn "doghand" about Blaze.

I remember last fall when my owner and one of his friends and I were pheasant hunting. On the way home, his friend asked him about Blaze and when she had "passed" (I don't know what that meant). What my owner said I'll always remember, just like I remember to put my nose into the wind when hunting pheasants! Lots of times my owner talks, and talks, and talks, and I don't remember when he says … but that day I did!

Savvy

He told his friend about a movie about dogs passing away and how he felt dogs had something like a soul in them. (I still don't know what a soul is, I know about soles on shoes that I used to chew.) He said he thinks dogs have like a "soul," 'cause they have more loyalty and love than many humans … He then scratched my head and told me Blaze would be really happy that I was here, 'cause if you love and lose a special dog, that dog would want you to pass on your love forward to another … in her memory.

Usually I take pen in paw and share with you all the fun things that happen to me in the animal and bird world. This week, I tried to sniffingly share my happenings from the human world. I don't understand all this soul stuff, but I'm glad I'm here.

I'll bark at you in April,

Savvy

Doggone Busy

It's been five weeks since I've taken pen in paw and told you about my life here on Lake Minnewashta. Someone once said, "It's a dog's life." I think they meant it was really a good life…cause I've got one!

Two exciting "canine cavorts" have happened to me since I last wrote. I learned how to jump off the dock and the boat into the water! Oh, I always knew how to swim, I guess that comes naturally to a lot of us. And I liked riding in the boat. And I would come into the water from the shore…but on July 14 all that changed, and now I can't wait to do a doggie belly flop off the dock.

Seems on that day Grandma, Grandpa, Shaelyn, Tyler and I took a boat ride over to the Terrace Park area to swim with cousins Eli and Olivia who were visiting their Grandpa & Grandma Dotson. Well, we anchored out by the swim ropes and my owner (Shaelyn & Tyler with life jackets) swam in. On his way back to the boat, my owner (you know, he's 67 and should know better) got tired, I think he quit walking on the bottom, he's too tall, and had to swim. He was treading water, I thought he was in trouble, and I just had to jump in to try to save him. I swam to him, he put his hands on me, and said he was OK, and we swam back to the boat. If you think I'm making this up for an extra dog biscuit, ask the grandkids.

Ever since then, when he and the grandkids jump off our dock, I follow them in! It's great fun to swim with them. On July 19, while playing in the water, I thought Olivia, even though she had on her life jacket, was in trouble. I grabbed her by the back of her hair and jacket and pulled her closer to shore. She bought me a whole bunch of treats! Let me tell you, those grandkids are so much fun to be around!

Last Saturday I got to walk in my very first parade, the Pioneer Days Parade in Milford. Actually, I led my owner all over the streets as we followed our Lakes News van and some carriers and their friends. Wow, were those people watching the parade smart! Everywhere we went, they would say, "Hey John, who is leading who?" or "We enjoy Savvy's columns (is that what this is?) more than yours!" That was Barkingly Beautiful sounds to my ears!

Oh, one more thing about this "owner" title. I've found out like a lot of lucky dogs have…that if the human you live with gives their heart to you, you "own" them…

and that's cool!

Well, that is it for now…you canines and canine owners, drop me a line if you get the time.

Swimmingly yours,

Savvy

My New "Doo"

Hello out there to all canines and their owners / friends who read my column when I take pen in paw. As many of you regular readers know (and for the benefit of summer "man's best friend" owners), I'm a 2 1/2 year old Golden Retriever who came to live with John and Mary Adams on the north shore of Lake Minnewashta in April 06. I try to write a column in the Lakes News every month cause the treats (chew bones and cheese slices) are grrrreat.

As you can see in the pictures, I went to the groomer last week! My owner decided my coat was getting too long for the hot summer. He tries to brush me at night, but it gets frustrating for us both! So ... for the first time I growling gave in and agreed to get "prettied up."

I went to the Doggy Motel and had Kelly Roberts groom and wash me. I sure feel quicker with that hair gone, bet I could almost catch a pheasant now! This was my first time getting groomed, and I liked the hair clipping much better than the bath, as you can tell! I know I've got it made, but I'd rather chase a goose in a stinky pond, or work up a pheasant from a muddy weed patch and then come home and jump off the

dock into our lake to get "clean" ... than take a bath! Thanks to Kelly ... people say I look sharp now with my shorter hair and dry coat. (I thought I looked sharp before!)

Dog-gone it,
have a grrreat week!

Savvy

My Point Of View
by Savannah Adams

Part Two

❀

What I
Really Think...

"Human Words" In A Canine World

This is kind of a slow time of the year for us all. As you know, most of the time I'm busy either hunting pheasants, helping my owner catch fish or roaring around the trails and woods. But winter has slowed us all down. Oh, I still get my two-a-day walks, but they're shorter and not as much fun. So, now I spend a lot of time lying by my owner's feet and working on my chew bones.

Because of that, I'm starting to hear a lot of human words this Golden Retriever doesn't understand. I'll share some with you and give you what I think they mean. When he isn't hunting or fishing (like now), he reads a lot of books and watches TV. That's where I hear these funny words.

• Blog — Isn't that like a frog? I ate two last fall and they were tasty (frog legs, you know).

• Stimulus — I think this is like when I'm training on my hunting moves … and I get a treat for doing good … This is my stimulus.

• Global Warming — My owner said those who believe this say it's caused by emissions. I said, like when I eat my dog food too fast and burp? Is that an emission? Warming? Have these people been stuck in drifts this winter, like me? I think it's a snow job!

• Mainstream — I swam in this last fall. We were pheasant hunting by this lake with a creek going into it … John T. shot a pheasant that sailed way out in the lake. As I retrieved it back, I got real muddy, so my owner took me to the creek and said, "Swim out in the 'main stream' to get clean!"

• Deficit — I'm facing deficits in my life now! Because I'm not exercising enough, my owner doesn't feed me my hunting rations. I get less meat … and that's a deficit to my appetite!

• War on Terror — I've been fighting this ever since I grew up. The "terrorists" I engage are skunks, geese, and squirrels.

• Tea Party — My best friend Lucy and I have these every week. We get together after we're done roaring around the neighborhood and have dog bones and water. A great tea party!

All these terms I hear on TV. One special one I learned when my owner reads his books is:

•A Great Read — I barked and told him I knew that one. A great reed to me is cat-tails by the slough that hide pheasants. He said he meant a very good and interesting book. That's about it from Oak Street. I've got new words to learn for my canine cavorting.

Stay in touch …

Savvy

Words I've Learned From Watching TV ...

Hello again from the north shore of Lake Minnewashta. This Golden Retriever has a lot to share with you this week. You see, I've learned many new words when my owner and I watch TV together. When we do watch TV, it's usually what they call "the news." I hear all these funny words … I growl at him to explain them to me … then he does, and then the fun begins! He tells me what he thinks the words mean … and I bark back at him what they mean in my everyday canine cavortings! It's like this —

• He and a friend were talking about who would control the house after the next election in November. I barked, "Tell me what kind of dog any politician owns, and I'll tell you if that politician is any good or not. As far as controlling the house, show me a dog that doesn't control their house!"

• We were watching TV News and they had a story about the terrorists in Afghanistan. (Have you seen how thin those dogs are over there? What a tough life.) Anyway, I snarled at that word terrorist and told my owner, "I've got personal Taliban I've got to deal with. Try negotiating with a goose trying to poop on your lawn or a squirrel swearing at you! Or a snapping turtle trying to hog my trail! But so far, I'm winning my war on terror."

• I don't think my owner believes much of that global warming talk. He told me lots of things cause emissions and then I knew what it was all about! You see sometimes when I eat too much or too fast … I get emissions! Now this being a family/dog paper, I was told I couldn't really tell you what my emissions do … but they're open ended!

• We watch many ads and he tells me that advertising is really important because businesses get the word out about their products and that helps inform people and helps support TV and papers like ours.

This is one word this Golden knows is ggrreat: I have two favorite ads I watch all the time! When they come on I start barking! Both have my dog family (Goldens) in them. Got to run now … see you on the screen or in the news!

Having good visions of you …

Savvy

Keep Talking ... Keep Writing ...
I Love It!

I'm writing again this week 'cause my owner had a lot of people ask him last week where my column was! In fact, in church, one of his friends told this story to a whole bunch of people! His friend said, "You can always tell, in the business drops where they leave the Lakes News each week ... If at the end of the week, there are papers left there, people know that my owner wrote an editorial and people after looking in the paper and finding his, some leave the paper there. But if Savvy writes her column ... all the papers are gone!" I love those words! They're ggrrreat!

Another friend told my owner in church that he and his grandson were out deer hunting this weekend, and their dog found a skunk, but disposed of it. However, before being subdued the stinker did his thing, and the hunters and dog spent much time getting deodorized! This Golden Retriever wonders, in the whole scheme of the animal kingdom, why God made skunks?

So we're sitting on our dock Sunday afternoon fishing. My owner's luck has been like a bouncing ball ... up and down, up and down. I "asked" him if there was anything exciting in the next two weeks that I could get doggone dizzy about and he said there were two days he thought I'd really like!

The first is Halloween. Now I growled, "I don't know what that is ..." He said you get dressed up and go trick or treating? I howled, "That would be easy ... I will wear my gold costume (coat) and go to houses and do tricks (like retrieving or staying) and get treats I can eat!! But he said the treats were candy, and I can't eat those!!

So I'm trying to get Halloween changed into "Dog's Night Out" with chew bones and meat as treats. Wouldn't that be scary?

In about 10 days, I get to start pheasant hunting. I guess we're going to start in a big CRP ground. I think (the way my owner shoots) that CRP means "Catch Rooster Please."

Stay in touch, I'll keep pen in paw,

Savvy

On Friends and Neighbors ...

Besides hunting for, and retrieving pheasants, this Golden Retriever has two other favorite pastimes. One is riding on the front of our boat when we go for boat rides on all our lakes. And the other is "helping" my owner catch fish. That's when we sit and "talk" (if he isn't catching Bluegills). But lately the 'gills have been biting, so our conversation is between casts.

"We" were talking this past weekend about all the similarities between dogs and humans. He asked me if I knew what a good neighborhood we lived in … and I barked that I did, 'cause my best friend Lucy (the Chocolate Lab across the street) and I were good neighbors. We take care of each other, like eating each other's food, looking out for each other when we're out playing, and finding neat things to roll in for each other, like dead fish and old muskrats.

"Well, Savvy," he said, "it's kind of the same way for us humans who live in the neighborhood." To have good neighbors, you have to be one." You try to help your neighbors out when they need a hand (or a paw). I try to help out when my owner and his friend Marv are fishing on our dock. They usually drop the Yellow Bass they catch on our dock when they go to put them in the fish basket (those fish twist and wiggle a lot). Three have fallen on our dock so far and I've saved two from going back in the lake … by catching them!

I've tried to be a good neighbor also by scaring off the geese who wanted to poop on not only our lawn, but on both of our neighbors'. Good neighbors look out for each other's property he told me. Maybe that's why I bark when I see anything suspicious in our neighborhood.

I think good neighbors are a lot like us dogs, they tease each other a lot. Sunday, he asked his neighbors, since they weren't catching a lot of fish, if they wanted those in his basket. They told him that would be OK, but couldn't he also clean the fish for them? Then they all had a good laugh!! On the way home, I told him, "Next time, you praise me for some hunting thing I do good and tell me I'm going to get a piece of steak, I'll bark at you, 'Prime rib, medium please, with a dog bone on the side'."

He then bent over, scratched my ear and said, "Savvy, keep on being a good neighbor, a good friend, and you'll have a great life …"

May all your neighbors be good …

Savvy

Bad Dreams

I've been so busy telling you what this Golden Retriever's been up to lately during the days … I've forgotten to tell you the funny things that have been happening at night! I've been having some wild dreams while I've been sleeping. I growled to my owner about it … He said he knew I was having trouble with dreams 'cause of all the weird sounds I've been making while asleep!

He told me humans dream a lot, but usually forget their dreams soon. I barked, "Dogs remember a lot longer than humans … and I remember the last two nights. And they've been dog-gone doosies!

The first dream was about my arch enemies … the geese. As you know, I've become the guardian of our beach area in the neighborhood, our neighbors let me roam on their lakefront when the geese try to come up and poop on our lawns; but I run 'em off! This summer, after I showed them who was boss, they've stayed away and it's been quiet. But they came up on me in my first dream! It was terrible, I dreamed I was hunting pheasants in this slough area and all of a sudden the sky became black with every goose, I think in the county, dive-bombing me! What could I do? The guys I usually hunt with (John T. and Steve S.) couldn't get their guns to work … and of course, my owner's shooting ability is so bad he couldn't hit a bull in the butt with a bulldozer so I was alone … without a chance.

The geese didn't attack me directly, flew over me and flew over me … and pooped on me! That's when I woke up … all squishy and smelly, and my owner said I was squealing … wouldn't you squeal, too!!

Then last night, I had a good dream! In fact, when my owner came in to wake me, he said I was smiling in my sleep! You would have smiled, too! I dreamed I was on a football field running and playing … All flat, no trees, no cover, and about 10 of the rodents I detest the most … squirrels … were there with me. As you know, squirrels bug me more than anything 'cause they yell and jabber swear words at me, then when I chase them to "straighten them out" … they run up the nearest tree and continue to cuss at me …

But in my dream, they had nowhere to run, no trees, and I started getting up close and personal with them … and all of a sudden, they weren't so smart anymore! And then, darn it … I woke up! But it sure was fun while it lasted …

See you soon … sweet dreams!

Savvy

I'm On A "Seafood Diet..."
I See Food, I Eat It!

Let me tell you of some mysterious happenings going on in my house here on the north shore of Lake Minnewashta. It involves food and how it just happens to wind up by me and then inside my tummy! Oh, I get good normal eats, dog food, chew bones, cheese slices, fish oil tablets for my coat, and if I'm really on good behavior, meat from dinner. So in terms of my subsistence … grrreat … I've got it made!

So why do I pull stuff like what happened Thursday night? Our family had roast beef the night before and my owner's wife had slices of the beef on a plate on the counter. I think she was going to make sandwiches … all of a sudden, the roast beef was on the floor by me and, of course, I ate it all! My side of the story is that our air conditioning just came on … and the breeze nudged the meat off the counter, and it fell right by me! They seem to think I knocked it off with my paw and nose and then devoured it! I hope you believe my side of this story!!

You see, my owner watches my weight. I am a hunting dog and he wants me to be in good shape all the time. I'm supposed to weigh in the 70s, I guess … to be sure I can move good in the field. I now weigh 77 pounds, so I'm getting trim for hunting (but please don't tempt me by putting food anywhere where I can smell it … 'Cause it will be your fault and not mine if I eat it!

My owner told me he was having cataract surgery Tuesday. I said, "Huh?" That's another human word this Golden Retriever doesn't have in his doggie diatribe. I growled at him and said, "All I know about that word gives me canine cause for concern. Does it mean cats are acting in a certain way?" I don't know many cats that would act the way I want them to —

He told me everything was fine and not to worry. Now, when we pheasant hunt, maybe he'll be a better shot since he won't have poor vision to blame for his causing me unemployment in the retrieving category … But I doubt it … I'm just glad his friends come hunting with us!! **That's it for this week …**

I think I smell some food cooking and I better investigate …

Savvy

Winter Games For Dogs!

All I've heard the past week, and all I've read in the Lakes News and The Canine Chronicle is about our University of Okoboji Winter Games in the Lakes Area. Now being a Golden Retriever, I don't exactly understand what they are; but I read the games schedule on page 3, and here are some events I think I could enter!

•Two Person "Best Shot" Golf Tourney. I don't know what golf is, but the two persons who are the best shots I pheasant hunt with are John T. and Steve S., so I think I could do well in this tourney! We could get a lot of "birdies."

•Bridge Party — I could play good in that 'cause I think it means you walk to a bridge, which I do every day with my owner, when the snow doesn't stop us. It's between Lower Gar and Minnewashta and I party with some of my dog friends and the animals that live by it!

•Family Fun at the Tube Hill — I've already done this event this winter! The grandkids and I went sledding over Christmas and I got tired chasing them down the hill on their tubes!

•Freeze Your Fanny Bike Ride — Ever been pheasant hunting when the wind chill is zero and the snow is up to my knees? And I'm on the pheasant scent? It's no wonder when I get home I plop on my rug and clean my toes out. I don't need to ride a bike to know when my fanny is frozen!

•Tour of Homes Poker Run — This sounds great! I get to go through a whole bunch of homes and meet many new canine friends. I hope they'll let me in!

•Marshmallow Man Blaster Shootout — I ate some marshmallows once when the bag fell on the floor … and I've been around much blasting during hunting season and when the fireworks go off – so whatever this is … I'm doggone ready to go!

•Polar plunge – I'll jump at the chance to do this … talk about easy. I plunge off the dock all the time with the grandkids when we're swimming, and in fact, I swam in real cold water a lot late this fall when I plunged into creeks and sloughs to retrieve five pheasants that had been downed.

Well, it should be fun! I'll see you all this weekend at The Games! I'll be the Golden Retriever (leading the "older" tall guy) on a leash!

Grrreat games to you!

Savvy

I've Got A Great Life!

It's that time again when this Golden Retriever takes pen in paw and fills you in on what's happening here on the north shore of Lake Minnewashta. My has been so good, and so busy that I've decided to you about my three favorite canine cavortings!

My funnest outdoor activity is pheasant hunting, but you all know that. Just being out-of-doors trying to out think the pheasant; running, scenting, pointing or flushing, retrieving … that's my favorite. And you know all about one of the two things I enjoy the most indoors … that would be eating! I get a steady diet of dry dog food, vitamin snacks, chopped meat, once in a while if I've been really good I can sample fish, beef or chicken, and of course cool water … So you see, I've got it made!

But lately I've been doing a lot of "reading." My owner and I spend some nights devouring books (I think that's like me eating). Actually, he reads and then he shares the pages with me. Sometimes we're sitting on the dock fishing or watching the sunset … and sometimes I'm laying at his feet by his recliner while "we" read.

He's funny, 'cause he reads books about three areas, two of which I don't know or care about! A dog doesn't understand politics … if I know what kind of pets politicians have, I'll tell you if you can trust them or not, (the politician, not the dog!). And mysteries? The only mysteries I care about are: Where are my dog buddies? Where is the pheasant hiding? Where is my food? You get the drift!

But lately he's been reading a lot about my favorite subject … Dogs! Grrrreat, it drives me barkingly bonkers to read all those stories about canines …

See you on the pages,

Savvy

Words Learned On The Dock … And A New Friend …

I was watching TV with my owner this week when an announcer said, "The dog days of summer are coming soon." Can you imagine how great that will be? Special days to honor us dogs! I asked my owner when it would be and how many special treats I'd get during those days. As usual, he was a dog-gone spoil sport, muttering something about dog days meaning "weather." Whether or not he knows what he's talking about, we canines deserve special days!

As a Golden Retriever, I have a hard time following human talk. Oh, I've got my basic commands down, but I always hear a new word and think what it means in canine conversation. Like last Thursday night, I'm sitting on the dock trying to help my owner and his friend Marv catch fish. When after about an hour, they said, "This is why they call it 'fishing.' and not 'catching'," I knew we were in trouble.

Because of the lack of keepers, the guys were throwing around words that went over my feathery tail. Later, I nuzzled my owner aside while we sat on the deck and growled, "Give me a run down on these words and how they relate to my doggie diatribe!"

• He said Amnesty meant you forgive someone for something wrong they had done (like being in this country illegally). I barked, "I know that. I'm always giving you amnesty when you don't feed me enough, or all the times you miss pheasants, and I forgive you."

• I always hear "How was your day?" He said that was a greeting among humans finding out what their friends had been doing all day. Again I howled, "Why don't you ever ask me that?" My day begins with our morning walk in the woods, then you go to work, so I go into the sunroom, plop down on the tile, and watch the lake. I either see my friends the ducks swim by, or the terrorists (geese) trying to figure out how to attack our beach and poop on it. Then you come home and we either go for another walk or do hunting exercises. That's my day. Grrrreat!

• I didn't understand lake drainage either, I growled. He tried to tell me how our lakes, when it rains a lot and the water gets higher, how a whole bunch of culverts not too far from here on Lower Gar Lake, make sure the water runs out and keeps a good level on our lakes. So we went for a boat ride down there! He showed the culverts to me (as I sit up front on the boat as always). Now I know. I wanted to jump out and swim through them, but old fuddy-duddy wouldn't let me.

I made a new friend last week on the trails! His name is Tucker, and he's a Wheaten Terrier. He was really cool. Tucker lives close by our walks so we barkingly agreed to try to drag our owners over about the same time daily so we could all get better acquainted!

Hope all goes well with you this week, I'll take pen in paw soon!

 **Savvy**

Human Words ... In A Dog's World

Sunday night, my owner and I are sitting watching TV, while he tried to help me finish this column. All these words I've been hearing both on the news and from "talks" we've had ... are not all registering in this canine's cerebellum (that's dog for brain, I think).

Because the fish haven't been cooperating (fish remind this Golden of many humans I know ... they wouldn't get in trouble if they kept their mouths shut). So I haven't been spending as much dock time as I'd like, and as a result I'm curled up at my owner's feet. I nuzzled my hunting nose into his hand and growled, "Give me a hand to understand all these new words that are filtering into my "wax-filled ears."

• I started with "polls and politics." He said humans ask other humans how they feel on issues of the day ... and politics is the art of governing, and right now, "There ain't much art." I growled, "Huh?" I do know parts of both words in my doggie diatribe – The "tics" part are nasty insects I don't get because my owner treats me each month with medicine, and if the little suckers get on me ... they fall off! As for polls, being a lady dog ... I don't have any use for them when I have to relieve myself!

• We heard on TV about a person being under house arrest. He tried to explain that as someone suspected of doing something bad ... can't move around like they're used to. I barked, "I know all about this ... you must have made up the word." Remember when I chased that wild turkey last week when you told me not to ... or when I rolled in that sweet-smelling fish ... or when I strayed away from you on the trail? After you scold me, bring me home, and put me in my room with a chew bone and water ... I feel like I'm under arrest in my house!"

• I asked my owner how come many times when I'm lying here by his feet, he's always watching stories about crimes, and what that was! He said it's about a good bunch of people who try to understand how bad people think and act, and then catch them. I kind of understood ... I said to him, "I know bad animals with bad minds ... like geese, squirrels, and a few wild cats (encountered while pheasant hunting) ... and I try to catch them, too!

**I'm learning a lot about the human world ...
hope these columns help you understand us dogs!**

 **Savvy**

A Dog's View of July 4th

Well, it happened again! My owner and I were sitting on our dock Sunday night. He wasn't fishing … he said he wanted the lake to settle down a little … (I think it was 'cause his fishing has been far better than his catching!)

We looked out to the west as the sun went down over the water, and he said, "Savvy, I'll bet you didn't know next weekend is July 4th … and what that means." I growled, "You know us canines … we try to figure out one day at a time, when we eat, where we walk, and if our owners will pay attention to us." "OK," he said, "let's 'talk' about some things you can relate to July 4th."

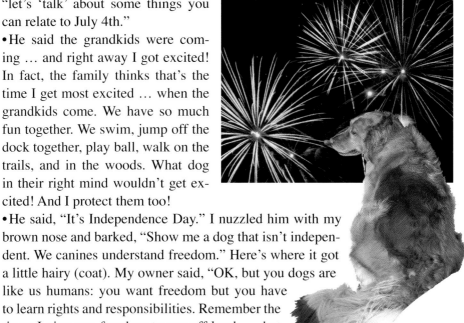

• He said the grandkids were coming … and right away I got excited! In fact, the family thinks that's the time I get most excited … when the grandkids come. We have so much fun together. We swim, jump off the dock together, play ball, walk on the trails, and in the woods. What dog in their right mind wouldn't get excited! And I protect them too!

• He said, "It's Independence Day." I nuzzled him with my brown nose and barked, "Show me a dog that isn't independent. We canines understand freedom." Here's where it got a little hairy (coat). My owner said, "OK, but you dogs are like us humans: you want freedom but you have to learn rights and responsibilities. Remember the times I give you freedom to run off leash … but you're learning you don't have the right to bother others …" That's being responsible.

I think I understand … it's my responsibility to stick my paw in his face every morning at 6:30am so he gets right up to take me on a walk! These July 4th words are fun!

• Then he said, "There will be a lot of fireworks and noise on July 4th. And I woofed, "A piece of cake (dogbone) …" Remember, how noisy it was last week with those storms? I'm to the point now where thunder and lightning don't bother me at all. In fact, Friday night, I was snoring so loudly my owner thought it was thunder!

But it wasn't always that way … when I was a pup, my owner worried 'cause noises bothered me so he took me to his friend Doug who knows a lot about hunting. Together, they worked with me, first making a sound by hitting on a pot, then shooting a rifle a long ways away, then a shotgun – all the time teaching me to retrieve. Pretty soon, I got so used to it, I hardly hear noise now and that's good 'cause my owner and his friends make a lot of noise hunting! I think you humans call it "much ado about nothing."

That's about it from Minnewashta. Hope you all have a happy holiday with your family and dogs!

Your Big Sparkler ...

Savvy

I Love Water!

Greetings again to you all from the north shore of Lake Minnewashta. I've been having a wet, wonderful time lately and wanted to shake the story on you! Last Thursday, grandkids Shaelyn and Tyler had friends Brenna and Lucas over for a swimming party. I, of course, joined in the fun!

The five of us were in the water over three hours! I jumped in behind them, and also jumped off the dock to go retrieve my hunting dummy, which my owner kept throwing and throwing. I've learned a new trick, how to come up the swim ladder steps by the boat; now I don't have to come up the bank to shake off on people! Boy, did I ever sleep good that night.

Water fun also means I get to ride in the front of the boat and greet all those people

and their dogs that we see. Usually I see two or three canines that are lucky like me. And talk about being excited! I was reading in my daily doggie diatribe that Aug. 26 is Dog Day! Just think … they set up a special day to honor us dogs. I was jumping up and down thinking I'd get some special treats when my owner threw cold water on my thoughts! He told me "Dog Day" might mean a day when it was really hot, like dog days of summer. But I growled I didn't care … doggone it, we should have a national day to honor all of us!

I'll take pen in paw again soon …
Have a gggrreat week.

Savvy

My Owner And Me ...

One of my favorite canine current happenings is to sit on our dock with my owner and "talk" about all the things that are happening in our lives. This usually takes place when we're fishing and, because he hasn't been catching many Bluegills lately, we've been talking a lot more. He tells me "that's why they call it fishing, and not catching."

Summer's coming and, dog-gone it, there are many fun things for this Golden Retriever to do! The first will start this weekend when the grandkids come to visit. We'll be jumping off the dock like we did last year and doing a whole bunch of swimming. And the bike trails will get visited by us all as Cyrus the Bulldog, Scout the Golden Retriever, and I search for the latest in toads, frogs, and bird and animal scents.

"We've" been doing a lot of reading and TV watching, too! I enjoy seeing the Golden Retrievers and German Shepherds that are used in airport security, drug

finding, and smelling out bad people in the war on terror. I asked my owner why those dogs are used, and he said, "It's cause their nose ... knows." And then he rubbed my brown nose!

I learned a new human word on the dock this weekend. It's called a "teachable moment" ... Now I admit I didn't have a clue what it meant but my owner and I were "talking" about those Goldens and Shepherds and how brave and loyal they were. He said, "Savvy, that's why all dog owners are so lucky, 'cause you give us so much more than we can ever give you back. Your love, loyalty and compassion that you show to those humans you "own" ... Makes all you canines far better than most of us," and then he scratched my head!

I hope you all have a ggrreat Memorial Day weekend.

See you soon,

Savvy

I'm Finding A Turkey For Thanksgiving ... Or A Pheasant Calling On The Phone!

Around Oak Street, the human talk has turned to "Thanksgiving." We dogs don't really understand what that means, or what "being thankful" means ... so I went to my doggie dictionary to find out what they're talking about!

So here's what this Golden Retriever thinks happens at Thanksgiving time. I guess the bird everyone eats is a turkey. Being a bird dog, I've had run-ins with wild turkeys. I see six every day we go for a walk through Henderson Woods. They live on some land across the road where we hunt. I once got in a scuffle with them ... I didn't know they could fly as well as they do (and they learned this Golden didn't like to gobble ... gobble!)

I thought we could hunt them like pheasants, but my owner said, "No" (he's always throwing cold water on my ideas) 'cause they have a season and we don't have a license to hunt them ... whatever that means! I guess I'll have to depend on turkey from the grocery store for my treats!

Now, more on the hunting scene ... this time for pheasants. I've got to let you in on a hunting secret ... please don't tell anyone. It seems like Steve S, who hunts with John T, my owner and me, has been bringing his cell phone with him as we hunt the fields and sloughs. The first time it rang, I stopped and wondered what was going on! He said, it's "business calls." But I've been watching and listening and I figured it out! It's one of two "groups" calling! I think it's pheasants on the phone and they're telling Steve, "Why don't you and Savvy's owner come over to where we roosters are ... you can't hit us anyway." Or it's the wives of the three guys I hunt with ... telling them to stop and bring home supper 'cause pheasant won't be on the menu!

Another true story! We're hunting Sunday after the snow and I'm having a ball smelling scent like wild and following pheasant tracks. My owner goes down this trail and yells back at John T and Steve S, "There are two rooster tracks here," and Steve yells back, "Are you sure it's not one that went down the trail and then turned around and went back the same way?" See what I have to put up with?

This hunting season has been so much fun I'm really thankful!

Nine days 'til Turkey Day ...

Savvy

My Point Of View
by Savannah Adams

Part Three

🐾

My Canine and Other Friends... (and enemies)

I Attend A Birthday Party ...
And Learn More About Dogs And Humans ...

This past week was a real exciting one for this Golden Retriever! I attended a birthday party for one of my owner's best friends; and in the process, I now know that humans and dogs have a lot in common!

On Sunday, my owner and I went up to see Dale and Sara Lundstrom, pictured, in Spirit Lake. It was Dale's 95th birthday and we had a ggrrreat time. We brought a present (Bluegills) and had cake and cookies! Even though I barkingly bribed them by telling everyone I had a birthday too (Dec. 5th) ... I couldn't get any cake! But I did end up with 2½ cookies ... and many back rubs.

Besides treats, one of the reasons I love to go there is to "check out" the kennels, where years ago the Lundstrom Golden Retriever puppies and their parents lived. Some puppies went down to central and southern Iowa (where I came from) and Dale, Sarah and my owner think I'm an original Lundstrom Golden 'cause I have three markings their dogs had: •a brown nose (instead of black), •a black diamond on my tongue, •and a high bone on my head. Even if I'm not, I've already adopted them as my kennel grandparents!

As we drove home, my owner and I "talked" about friends. I know Dale and Sarah have been his friends a long time, 'cause he tells me a lot about their Goldens – and the support their furniture business gave him when this paper started.

He said, "Savvy, good friends are very important in all our lives. They are there for you when you need them, and won't let you down. You should never forget them."

I began to understand and growled that I had good friends and I would never forget them either. (Dogs have better memories than humans anyway.) Dogs have an advantage though, 'cause they can have canine and human friends!

As we went down the road in his SUV, me sitting in "my" seat up front right, he went on ... "Savvy, some you meet will be friends, like the dogs you meet on the trail or those canines that write you letters ... A few won't be (like squirrels, skunks, and a few canines who always bark at you or won't play with you.) And then there will be your good friends."

This Golden knew right then what he meant and I barked, "I know! I have three good canine friends: Lucy, Cyrus and Scout. And four good human friends … Kelly and Shawn Roberts of the Doggy Motel, where I stay when my family is gone; and Steve Schmidt and Jon Tonsfeldt, whom we pheasant hunt a lot with!"

Here's hoping you have good friends … and are one too!

Savvy

Me & My Best Friend

Hello out there, canines and canine owners. It's time for me to again take pen in paw and tell you about life on Lake Minnewashta. Actually, this week I'm going to tell you about a really neat dog that happens to be my best friend! Lucy is a Chocolate Lab who lives with Ron & Kris Walker, right across the street from us. As you can see in the picture above, our tongues are usually hanging out, cause we play so hard together!

Lucy is a lot older than I am, she's three and I'm just 1 1/3 years old! We're both hunting dogs, Lucy usually goes duck hunting and I love to pheasant hunt. In growling

with her, we found out that both our masters are lousy shots, and that we often have to save the day by retrieving the few game birds they were lucky enough to shoot at. I think sometimes my owner scares them so badly they fall to the ground and I can catch 'em! Seriously, my owner and his friend Scott from Madelia take me hunting often. I had to catch three on the ground for them last fall, and whenever they miss (90% of the time) I turn around and give them a dirty look! Lucy has similar horror stories about being in a duck boat, falling out, and seeing ducks 5 minutes before Ron does!

But it's not hunting where we have the most fun…when our owners get home from work, whichever lets us out to go for a walk or play in the yard, the other will see our buddy through the window and make such a ruckus we're sure to get let outside. You can set your doggy watch on Oak Street that at 5-6 PM and 6-6:30 AM we're on the lookout for our best friend! As you can see above, we wrestle a lot (I

think I'm getting the worst of that deal) and we play tag throughout our yards. We were going so fast last week and I wasn't watching, and I ran klunk right into a basketball goal pole! Boy, I saw two dog biscuits in my eyes for several minutes.

I hope all you dogs are fortunate like I am to have such a good friend to play with. Lucy's a toot! Drop me a line and let me know about your "buddy."

**Barkingly yours
for now,**

Savvy

Canine Capers

Hello out there, to all canines and canine owners! It's April, so here's my latest dog delvings into what's happening in my neighborhood on Lake Minnewashta. There's so much going on…it's been grrreat…

Do you remember last month when I got that neat letter from that part golden retriever who got adopted by a great family from the lakes area. I am so happy for him!! People always say, "It's a dog's life." Part of that is true when we dogs have humans that love us like we love them!

Now on to something not as nice…and that's geese! I am so mad at them! It all started last summer when they tried to come on our lawn and poop on it! My owner let me chase them away, and that is so much fun! One time last summer I swam out to chase three away, and one stayed in the water, and we started to get snooty with each other; but then he "fowled out" and flew!

I was talking to my best friend Lucy (the chocolate lab across the street) and we both agreed that when the geese hiss at us and squawking, they use worse language than squirrels do! In fact, I couldn't repeat any of it in this dog rated family paper!

Last fall my owner and I were coming back from hunting. He let me out of the van by our house, and I took off down Oak Street! Our neighbors were in their front yards and said it looked like fur flying! I caught a goose who I don't think could fly but was trying to get to the lake. By the time my owner got there, I was sitting on the goose's rear, and he was staring back at me! They said we could have goose for dinner, but I had to let him go and go home. Boy, was I mad at my owner!! But it was kind of like hunting pheasants…when he misses them, I have to try and catch them anyway.

Then last week while walking on the trail there were three geese on a pond off the trail. I went swimming after them…boy, the water was cold! In fact, my fur was frozen till I got home and dried out. I am so glad all the snow has melted and I can meet all the nice people and old dog friends on the paths again.

I think the ice went off our lake April 12…that's really good cause now I can help my owner fish. It's fun catching fish. I put them in my mouth and measure whether they're big enough to keep or not. Kind of a "Retriever Rule" you could call it.

Golden Days to you all,

Savvy

My Buddy and Me ... Part II

About a year or so ago, when I started taking pen in paw and sharing my neat life here on Lake Minnewashta with you, I told you about my best dog pal, Lucy. Lucy is a chocolate lab who lives right across the street and owns Ron and Kris Walker.

In the past month, Lucy and I have been busy with some crazy canine capers! I've been keeping track of them so I could tell you all about our neighborhood news:

Two weeks ago, Lucy and I were playing outside, our owners and neighbor, Marv Mettler, were visiting on the street, watching us. Karen Mettler came out to see what the guys were talking about. She left her house door open ... We roared in, chased their cat Raider around, looked for something to eat and would have stayed longer, but the adults figured out where we went ... and found us!

Lucy and I have a deal worked out. Whenever one of us is out, the other looks out the window and makes such a ruckus, we get let out! But I must tell you, Lucy has been a very greedy guest twice this past week. She was outside, came to our door looking for me. My owner let her in. She then proceeded to go into my room and eat all my food out of my dish! Once was OK between best friends ... but twice?

I've had a couple of strange animal run-ins too! My owner and I came out our door April 30 for our 10 p.m. walk. I took one step outside and here were two big deer! One was on our driveway, the other on our front lawn. Lucky for them, I was on my leash. As it was, they took off down Oak Street, their hooves going clackety-clack on our cement. Boy, that was scary.

But speaking of scary ... I met a new creature last Saturday. As we started our walk into Henderson Woods, I hadn't taken ten steps on the trail when I smelled something weird. I turned and went toward this big green, rough, bumpy thing in the woods. I started to sniff it out, and as my owner yelled at me, this big head and neck came out of the shell and took a swipe at me! My owner was so mad at me! He scolded me and told me that if a snapping turtle got my nose ... it would be really, really bad! So I'm leaving those green bumps alone. (I was told this turtle was probably laying its eggs back by a pond and I won't see her again.)

Well, as you can see, it's been a busy month for us here. Hope you've been g-g-great! If any of you canines have had exciting times like me, drop me a line.

Golden days to you,

Savvy

Pests In My Life!

No sooner did I take pen in paw two weeks ago and tell you how quiet it was around here since the grandkids left … than I started getting busy being hassled by some dog-gone irritating animals.

All the times I've gone hunting, I've never run into a skunk. My owner gets nervous about it … in fact, he told me he has a plan if I get stinky … He bought some anti-skunk shampoo, and my best friend Lucy told me when she ran into a skunk,

her owner took her to get a wash job and she smelled better, so I was ready!

Well, June 5th, my owner and I were practicing some hunting drills on land he hunts on … when I noticed the grass moving by the fence, so I moved in for a closer look, and guess what? There was a black and white "kitty" about five feet away, and it moved around like the picture … Lucky for me, my owner saw it and got me out of there, but as I backed off it started smelling terrible … was I a lucky dog! (I don't like shampoo either.)

I've barked at you before about what pests geese are. Now I've got a new job … I'm the guard dog for our lawn and three of our neighbors! When geese try to get out of the lake and poop and mess up our lawn, I get to chase them off! Last time it happened, three of them came up on our neighbor's beach. I went in the

water and two flew, but one turned and came after me! He tried to peck me while I was in the water, but when he tried to get my face I grabbed at him … He yelled

some goose profanity and flew away! That was gggrreat!

Then last week twice while taking our hike on the bike trail, I almost came face to face with snapping turtles. The first time, I was about 10 yards ahead of my owner and came upon this big creature that looked like a green rock, but he moved his head and my owner yelled, "No" at me. I think everyone to the Sawmill Bridge heard him! I know I did and got my nose out of there.

Well, that's about it from the north shore of Minnewashta.

I hope you have no pests in your life this week!

Savvy

Doggone It ... Summer's About Over!

Hello to all you canines, canine owners and readers! This Golden Retriever is a little sad that summer's ending, but I've got a lot of news to share with you!

I've got a boyfriend! If you promise not to tell anyone, I'll tell you more! His name is Zeus and he lives in Minneapolis, so we have a long distance romance. He comes down and visits our neighbors here on Minnewashta. He brings his owners and their children with him.

He's about a year younger than me, and a golden, too, so you can imagine our running around together had tongues wagging here on Oak Street! There were stories about the older woman and the younger guy. We're shown in the picture above, Zeus on the left, and me as we discussed possible marriage and puppies the last time he was here. But I think we have to stay sweethearts cause I heard one of Zeus' "grandchildren" talking about the possible marriage and puppies. He said, "I don't think Zeus and Savvy can have puppies 'cause they've both been 'noodled' " ... whatever that means!

Zeus is a city dog and doesn't hunt, but is a great family dog. I've tried to have him help me when I jump in the lake and work on my retrieving. In this picture, and usually, Zeus left, swims along with me and "tries" to help me bring the dummy back to my owner.

We have so much fun in the water together! This weekend, he'll be here and we can roar around! The most exciting news for this weekend is that our grandkids (all six) will be here so I'll have plenty of fun on hikes around the lakes, fishing, swimming, toad hunting (they may not let me go though, 'cause last time I ate a frog), and much more!

Hope all of you have a grrreat Labor Day weekend.

Bark at you soon!!

Savvy

I Got Skunked!

November 23rd is a day that I have written in stinky-ink in my dog diary. During the last three years doing my favorite activity of pheasant hunting, my owner warned me to stay away from black and white animals known as skunks. Oh, I've seen them from a distance, but never before up close and personal!

Anyway, we were hunting this CRP ground west of Milford and I had just flushed up a hen. (I told you before … pheasants smell the same to my nose, whether they're a Mr. or a Mrs.) I turned the corner on the trail of a rooster … and came face to face with this skunk! 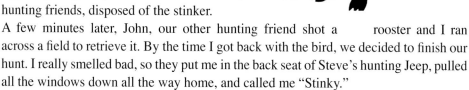 So here's what happened … He hissed some profanities at me so I tried to grab him! I got his face, but he swung around and boy did I get a snout full of stink!! I came running over to my owner coughing and wheezing and getting away from that animal! Steve, one of our hunting friends, disposed of the stinker.

A few minutes later, John, our other hunting friend shot a rooster and I ran across a field to retrieve it. By the time I got back with the bird, we decided to finish our hunt. I really smelled bad, so they put me in the back seat of Steve's hunting Jeep, pulled all the windows down all the way home, and called me "Stinky."

Talk about embarrassing!! But imagine this … on the way home, John (talking about the pheasant he shot) said, "We didn't get skunked!" I jumped up to the front seat and growled at him, "You may not have, but I did!"

 When we got home, I knew how bad I smelled so I got real quiet while my owner wetted me down and gave me two shampoos with some anti-skunk shampoo he had gotten from our vet. It was real good, in fact by late that night people wanted me around again!

December 5th was my birthday! I turned four and had a great birthday party Dec. 4th. We went hunting, I got to flush and retrieve two and got great birthday treats from Steve and John. (I think I'm supposed to share with my owner. I don't know if I will or not.) And I got some new chew bones from the guy that keeps me smelling good.

Have a grrreat Christmas! It's doggone good being four … and not being stinky!

Savvy

38

Of Animals ... And People

It's time to take pen in paw and visit with you again! According to my owner, judging by the comments he gets when I write an editorial compared to his; I should be writing every week ... and he can write monthly! As I barked this summer ... "It's a dog's life," and that means it's a good life!

I've been coming across a lot of animals and people lately. Now the people have been grreat ... the canine consensus is still out on the animals!

The animals around here keep me on my paws. In the past week on our trail walk, I ran into that snapping turtle I told you about this spring. I think he was on his way back from the pond to the lake. Anyway, I tried to get in his face, but remembered before and pulled back before he could grab my nose. Then on my late night walk we saw a skunk, but I really listened to my owner 'cause I don't want to tangle with him and end up in the bathtub!

In a couple weeks, I can pheasant hunt again! This is my favorite time of the year. We've been working out to get ready, me retrieving my pheasant scented dummy and brushing up techniques. I wish my owner could practice shooting so I'd get more work! Actually, I hunt two different areas, in the fields around here and down at a game preserve. I didn't know why they called it a game preserve 'til I went hunting with my owner, his friends Scott and Shawn. The way those guys shoot, wild game will be preserved! Actually, I'm glad he brings Shawn, 'cause he can shoot pretty straight and then I get to retrieve.

Around here, there are these rooster pheasants by the trail. I flush them up and they cackle and laugh at me and fly across the road. What they don't know is that the fields they fly into are the ones my owner hunts, so I'll see them soon!! Ha-ha.

My owner and I had a good talk one night last week down on our dock, while we were fishing. He was sad 'cause two of his friends' special dogs had passed away. One was 16 years old and had been with the family all that time; the other dog was eight and had gotten sick. Their owners, because they loved them, didn't want to see them suffer any more. I told my owner I didn't understand all that stuff. He told me all I had to know was that every dog gives so much more to its owner than the owner ever can return; that he thought us dogs had something like a soul; and that there was a movie about dogs passing & going to heaven. Then he scratched my head and thanked me for being here. I guess I understand now. That's it from Oak Street. You canines and canine owners drop me a line if you have time.

Falling ... for you,

 **Savvy**

A Lesson Learned!

My owner and I were sitting on the dock last Tuesday night. We were "talking" about humans and canines … He said, "Savvy, as you grow older (in dog years) you have, and will meet many canines, humans, and animals. Most you will like, and treat with respect; but there will be a few who will push you (and bug you) to a point that you will push back. They will draw a line (with their paw) in the sand, and you will cross it. You will show them you can't be dogged!

I really didn't understand all that talk, but the next morning I learned up close and personal what he was jabbering about. We walk at least twice a day in different wild areas. It's cool … not quite as great as pheasant hunting, but fun, and it keeps me in shape.

Wednesday morning, we walked past this pond, all smelly, green, with a big tree that had fallen down right in the middle. As we went by, there were three geese sitting on the tree. (You know me with the geese that poop on our lawn). I acknowledged them with a glare, trying to give limited respect, even though it wasn't due! They jabbered some profanity at me, but I kept on walking. I was proud of myself.

About 20 minutes later, we came back by. They were still there, and starting hurling insults at me … and all canines. They used language I can't repeat in a family paper. I got mad, jumped in the slough and started swimming towards them. They all flew away (I thought). By the time I got back to shore, my owner was mad! I was pretty wet and stinky … I started shaking myself off. And then, and then, one of the geese came back and landed on the log.

He was so nasty! Making noise, and he made a naughty gesture towards me. I think you humans call it "giving the bird." Can you imagine, a bird doing that to me? Anyway, I got so mad I jumped back in, swam all the way to the log where he sat waiting for me. I think he foolishly thought I wouldn't cross that line he drew …

but I did! He stayed there taunting me 'til I got there. I grabbed him by the rear. He flew away with a sore butt and a few less tail feathers!

I think I learned a lot about behavior last week … human and animal. Treat people (and dogs) with respect, until they show you that you shouldn't.

Have a gggrreat week!

Savvy

A Canine Christmas
at my Home on Minnewashta

Like all canines and humans... I was dog gone glad when it quit snowing Saturday night. I had fun in the snow as you can see. I was trying to get out of a drift which I had gone into chasing a rabbit! Holy hunting hound... that snow was deep!

Snow!

I also enjoyed "tubing" with the six grandkids on Christmas. Actually I ran down the hills as they slid down... 'till I got really tired. But I didn't like the snow cause my owner said we can't go pheasant hunting anymore 'cause it's too deep… what a bummer!

Cats

Our house was really rocking over Christmas! And, for the first time, we had felines.

(I think that's a fancy word for cats.) Kittens Gibbie, came with Cyrus the bulldog, and Willow, who came with Scout, the Golden Retriever. My owner had told our family that I didn't like cats... based on my stand off with a neighbor cat Radar, and my chasing one up a tree last fall. So the grandkids who "owned" the kittens, Mya and Olivia, were worried...Well, I fooled everyone! I "talked" to Cyrus and Scout and found out they "tolerated" their fellow pets, so I decided to basically ignore them. In the picture I'm asking them why they got to get up on our couch... when I can't!

Christmas Presents

I got some wonderful gifts for Christmas. And my owner's friend, Tom Clary, of Milford Manufacturing, made me a personalized windchime! You canines should tell your owners

to see Tom and they can put you on your own decorations! My best friend Lucy gave me canine cookies. They were gr-rreat, but I was nice and shared them with Cyrus and Scout. It was barkingly beautiful to have Christmas decorated cookies of our own... canine style! The grandkids gave each of us dogs our own stockings with dog bones in them!

So, you can see, I had a happy holiday and hope you did, too!

 Savvy

On Meeting Mean Critters ...
And A True Story

Holy hounds ... there's so much going on around here I've got to write again to keep you updated on all my escapades!

I've had interesting experiences on two of my early morning walks on our trail. Last Tuesday, my owner and I had just gotten going when we came to the part where there's a smelly slough on my left and across the trail to my right is Lake Minnewashta. I noticed something big, green and mean off the trail, so I started to smell it out ...

Out came a big gnarly head with teeth that looked like it wanted to bite me! My owner pulled me back just in time. I don't think snapping turtles like Golden Retrievers!!

I couldn't talk to the turtle 'cause all he did was make a scary sound like a gasp at me! My owner had warned me about them before. I asked him why the turtle wanted to leave his slough and cross towards the lake. He said that maybe the turtle was tired of being a big fish (turtle) in a little pond and wanted to try to be a little fish (turtle) in a big pond! Dog-gone if I can understand that human talk!

Then Wednesday morning, I couldn't sleep, so about 6:30am I went in and stuck my paw in my owner's face and told him it was time to go! We took the back gravel trail through the woods. I was off leash and down by the Bike Trail Bridge.

I smelled something weird down by Lower Gar, so I went down the side of the hill, and there it was! It was an oposum, and my owner told me it wasn't playing 'possum (whatever that meant). It just laid there and grinned at me. My owner said, "Savvy come." So I got out of there. He told me possums are nocturnal creatures ... I growled, "Huh?" He said that means they come out and play at night, and if you see one during the day, they might be sick. I told him, "Does that make us dogs dayturnal 'cause we play all day?" He told me to quit "playing" with him.

Lots of people ask us when we're out for walks if what I write is true ... and I can barkingly tell you it is!!! And the following story really happened Wednesday night! My owners and I were sitting on our deck trying to cool off in the heat. (Remember last week I told you about me getting in the doghouse rolling in that smelly fish two doors down.) Well, from two doors down came a friend of the family and said he wanted to buy me a bath 'cause he was the one who left the dead fish on the beach! He had just gotten to the lakes, read my column, and knew he left the stinker there!! What a nice guy, but I nuzzled my owner aside and growled, "This is a great guy and a generous offer … but I'm not having another bath." Thought you'd enjoy this!

I got a nice letter this week from Abby inviting me to a party Sunday. Think I'll put my owner on a leash and bring him along. She sounds like a fun dog to meet and the party sounds like a good time! See you there!

That's it for now, see ya …

Savvy

Toads ... Fun In The Water

What a woofwunderful week it has been here on the north shore of Lake Minnewashta. As usual, it's non-stop fun! Three of the grandkids from Des Moines came up Wednesday and that night we went toad hunting!

Last year when they stayed, we would go out at nights looking for toads. We didn't find any then.

We did Wednesday night ... You should see us!! Four grandkids, my owner and I with a big lantern walking up and down Oak Street at 10:00pm! I don't get the fuss with toads. I checked out the one we found with my hunting trained nose and guess what ... nicely put, I don't think the toad had used deodorant for a couple of days. Smelling them is not a highlight of my night life. Now frogs, that's a different matter.

My owner told me some people eat frog legs – so several times this summer, when I've been down by the lake, I gulped down one. I can't say much for the taste, at least they smelled better than Mr. Toad who, by the way, is now living in the Toad Hotel in our garden!

Then Thursday, we went swimming over on West Okoboji! I've only swum there once before so it was great. We anchored in Millers Bay and the grandkids jumped in. Naturally, they called me to come in. So I jumped in, not from the swim platform, but from the middle part of the boat. Next time, I'll do my high dive off the top! I was so tired when I got home I took a dog (cat) nap!

I'd like to thank those dogs who have been writing me "Letters to Savvy." I'm really glad they read my column each week to their owners and we can together spread our canine conversation all over the area!

Stay cool and be kind to your four legged friends!

Savvy

The Bad ...

My owner always tells me life is full of surprises, both good and bad. Whether you're a human or a Golden Retriever, how well you do is how you adjust to the surprises that come your way! I'm here to tell you, this hunting hound learned that lesson this week!!

Let me tell you about the Bad ... Tuesday after he was done delivering papers, my owner tells me, "It's time to start your pheasant hunting work-outs." I evidently haven't convinced him yet that I can just go and start hunting when the season starts. I growled that once you're a hunting dog, you remember what to do when you get in the field. The nose goes to the ground, you start going back and forth through the area your humans are hunting, you "zone in" on the birds, point or flush them, and hope your hunters shoot straighter than my owner – so you can retrieve. Anyway – enough of the fine points – we're out practicing, (what choice did I have?) on this private land we hunt and I had just finished this weed patch when I noticed a vaguely familiar smell to me brown nose. It was a fragrance I had not inhaled since last fall. I remembered where it was coming from!! Around the corner of the weeds came Mr. Skunk! (Remember my last run-in, when hunting last November with Jim T and Steve S. I got sprayed, but Steve subdued the stinker.) Well, this

time it wasn't hunting season so my owner only had his commands and leash. Big deal! Even if he had been armed, I don't think Mr. Stinker would have been held to account. As it worked out, I did have the good sense to listen to him, and get out of that smelly situation. "We" came home, his SUV got deodorized and I had two anti-skunk shampoos before I was deemed appropriate to live inside again ... Bad – and the other bad thing is that I might meet Mr. Stinker again this fall! I hope he moves ...

I hope your weeks aren't bad!

Savvy

On Being In The Doghouse ...
Boating ... A New Name And New Friend

Greetings to all you from the Golden Retriever that lives on the North Shore of Lake Minnewashta. It's been so dog gone busy around here I don't know where to begin this canine conversation!

I guess I'll start with the bad news ... I've been in the doghouse the last couple of days, through really no fault of my own. First off, the grandkids were all here over the 4th, and so I spent hours with them swimming in the lake – grrreat! My owner thought I needed a bath after all that waterwork, so he tried to give me one. You know how I hate baths, and how badly he gives them! Shampoo in my eyes, too much water, you know the story. Anyway, I guess I didn't pass the smell test so he took me out to The Doggy Motel and Kelly gave me a bath.

Now that's a little more like it. In a big tub, gently shampooed, brushed, I felt like a pampered pooch. So I come home, we're going for a boat ride and just before I jump in the boat, this fragrant aroma of rotten fish reaches my trained-to-smell-everything nose. Never mind that it's two houses down; it smells so juicy I jump off the dock, head straight down the beach and roll and roll in the smelly deceased from the deep of Minnewashta! It seemed like only a minute of sheer pleasure before I realized I was in deep doggie doo-doo (if you know what I mean) I snuck

home, amid reprimands of "bad dog" and "stinky."

I growled at my owner to get over it, all dogs do it, and I'll probably sin again, if the smell is rotten enough!

On the golden (bright) side, I've had a ball out in the boat lately. It's so cool to have boaters wave at me, call my name, and I often see dogs riding on the fronts of their boats like I do. I nuzzled my owner while we were on West Lake Sunday, and a boat came by with a small dog wearing a life jacket. I said, "What's up with that dog ... a life jacket?" He told me not all dog families can swim like hunting dogs do. He said, "Remember Maggie the Beagle from Des Moines and how she fell off our dock and almost sank like a rock until we

pulled her out?" I said I remembered (we dogs remember about everything) and that I was glad I loved the water.

I met a new friend Sunday! While we were walking on the trail down by the bridge between Lower Gar and Minnewashta, I met another Golden, named Shelby. She had along the two people she owns so we had a good growl fest. Shelby lives in Spirit Lake, this was her first time on our part of the trail, and she told me she wants to come back to explore the woods with me and learn more about turtles, sloughs, anything with a smell. She's three and I'm four so us girls had a lot in common! It's always fun to meet new friends on the trail.

Hope your times and memories are golden …

Savvy "Stinky"

Pheasants Forever Youth Hunt ...
A Great Time!

Saturday, Oct. 23rd, I had a blast! I went with my owner to the Dickinson County Pheasants Forever Youth Hunt. There were 55 young hunters there. They were guided by Pheasants Forever members and their hunting dogs (that's me).

I made a new friend! We took Lucas Hoover and his grandpa Jack Eichman with us. We worked hard, saw many birds, and Lucas bagged his first pheasant! On top of that, it had the longest tail feather, 21¼ inches, winning Lucas top prize in that contest at the hunt!

That was so cool, I was hunting this weed patch and flushed up a big rooster. Lucas made a good shot, and the bird came down running. It took me about a block and a trip into a water filled ditch, but I found him for Lucas! The rooster's long tail feathers came off in my mouth as I was catching him, so in the picture I'm asking Lucas if he managed to save them for the contest ... and he did!

About noon, we all got back to the PF hunt headquarters, which was at Rod Sheldon's acreage just east of Milford. The lucky guys got to go and eat hamburgers, hot dogs, and pop, while I had to stay in our SUV! I was so tired I took a nap ...

Then "bang," "bang," and "bang!" I woke up and jumped up on my front seat. I saw many of the young hunters shooting at these orange birds that were flying. They really flew fast and were small! My owner came back and told me the youth were trap shooting at "clay pigeons." Those were weird birds; I don't know if I'd like to try to flush and retrieve them!

It's really good that the week ended so good and that I "officially" start pheasant hunting next Saturday with John T., Steve S., and "Never Hit" (that's my owner), 'cause I was in the doghouse around here since Tuesday! Seems like Tuesday noon, my owner's wife brought home a lovely pork sandwich and potato salad for her lunch.

She placed them on the kitchen counter, and went into the other room for a minute. Do you know what happened? We had a strong wind that day, the window was open and the food blew on the floor, so what else could I do, but eat the whole meal (never had potato salad before) 'cause I'm sure she would have thrown it away and I didn't want to waste good food!

Out of the doghouse … into the weed patch. See you soon!

Savvy

Getting Skunked Again ...
And Understanding Thanksgiving

Pardon the pun ... but last Wednesday I was in the "doghouse" again. You see, John T, my owner and I were pheasant hunting (what else is new?). It was a good day and I was tracking this one pheasant when I came across a place in the snow that had just been occupied by a skunk. Long story short ... the pheasant wasn't by the creek where I thought he was ... and all of a sudden the smell on the snow drew me over there! What is there about skunks and me?

I rolled and rolled in it ... and it smelled so good (to me) ... Boy, was my owner mad at me! First of all, I got John T's SUV a "little" stinky, he told me it smelled OK by Thursday, though. My owner told me John's SUV was almost an antique ... I growled "Huh?" He explained an antique was something older and valuable. I told him, "You're an antique to me ... except when you get upset with me."

When we got home after hunting, I had to have a shampoo to get the stink off me! It works well ... I missed getting Steve S's SUV stinky ... He wasn't with us ... I think he was home answering his cell phone!

In two days, we're all going to celebrate Thanksgiving! Here's what I think Thanksgiving means, to this Golden Retriever:

T – Turkey, hope I get a few leftovers this weekend!

H – Hunting ... enuf said!

A – All the great friends I've made this year, from canines to companions to conversationalists (letter writers)

N – Nutrition ... see all I do think about is food!

K – Kids, from the grandkids to all those new young friends ... they're the greatest!

S – Snow, don't like it! It slows me down hunting and moving ... thankful when it melts!

G – Gobble, gobble ... Don't like wild ones!

I – Insomnia ... Never have it ... Thankful I can sleep where and when I want to! (Especially after hunting ... I lie down, close my eyes, and zzzzz!)

V – Visitors ... I always greet them at our door with a bark and a wag of my tail ... and for those who let me ... a lick by my big tongue!

I – It's a great life that I'm thankful for!

N – Need to get some more "Letters to Savvy" ... Love it ... write when you can!

G – Got to go now ... I smell a pheasant ... somewhere.

Happy Thanksgiving!!

Savvy

Have You Ever Been "Badgered" ...
And New Words For My Vocabulary ...

Wow (or Bow-Wow), did I have a busy week! Last Tuesday, we were hunting ... I had just retrieved a rooster that John T hit ... when my owner missed two in a row that I flushed. He is so funny ... after the third one flew away, he started blaming his gun. The same gun that he was bragging about two weeks ago when he was having better luck! You figure that one out, this Golden can't! Anyway, on the third one he missed, it flew across the creek and on our way back on the other side of the ditch, both he and John T called me over to some weeds like a small muskrat house 'cause they thought that the pheasant was hiding in it ... I started smelling and got a whiff of some weird animal. I backed out and it started growling with a growl I'd never heard!

John T thought I was growling at a pheasant so I went back in the patch ... I stuck my snout down a hole and out came a canine curdling growl and a badger! Af-

ter seeing one ... I don't care if I ever see another! I've had some strange run-ins this fall with some cunning critters! Oh, by the way ... the badger won't be badgering anyone else!

Thursday, the grandkids all came for Thanksgiving! I got a few slivers of turkey (not as much as my stomach was hoping for). Saturday, my owner took Eli, Isaac, Olivia and Tyler out to target practice with their air rifles. Wow — can those kids shoot straight! I growled at my owner that he should take lessons from them! "We" put up targets and placed cans in trees. After they hit the cans, which fell out of the trees, I got to retrieve them! It wasn't exactly a pheasant retrieve ... but it was fun! A little "ruff" around the edges ... if you know what I mean!

"We've" been watching the news, my owner and I. I heard some new words this week that I've figured out ... what they mean in my doggie diatribe ... Here goes —

• "Lame Duck Congress" — My owner told me this is about people in Washington meeting now to vote on laws ... when many of them won't have a job in 30 days. I said, "Huh?" – To me it's about hunting ... If there's a lame duck somewhere ... I'll get a chance at a retrieve!

• "Unemployment" — My owner told me there are a lot of people who want to work ... and can't find jobs. That is so sad and I can relate to that. In our canine world, all dogs want families to love, and to love them. And hunting dogs want wild birds to scent. That's our job … to love, and for some of us … to hunt. So if either of these things wouldn't happen, we'd be unemployed.

I'm taking my pen out of my paw now …

hope your week's are as busy and as good!

Savvy

My Point Of View
by Savannah Adams

Part Four

Stuff I forgot in the First Three Parts!

A Dog's View Of "Happy New Year"

You know, I just got that "Merry Christmas" figured out … and now I start hearing something like "Happy New Year." So here's what I think that means to this Golden Retriever! And what I'll hope to do in the New Year.

H — Hunting, my favorite thing to do … This has been my most fun fall ever!

A — All the new friends I made this year: Canines on the bike trail, canines who wrote me letters, and two cool guys we hunt a lot with … Steve Schmidt and John Tonsfeldt.

P — Protect our grandchildren … Both walking on the bike trail or in the water swimming.

P — Pretty great to be with my family at this my third winter at the lake.

Y — Yes, it's a dog's life … and I love it!

N — Not warm enough for me. I want the deep snow to melt so I can hunt more!

E — Ever watch TV? I do! My owner and I watch it, and my favorite "program" is any commercial with golden retrievers in them!

W — Worst creatures I've met … Geese are No. 1 – They "mess" on our lawn, and it's not an accident. But I chased them off this fall … (actually got in a fight with one of them) and they didn't come back! Squirrels are bad (I can understand what they yell at me when I run them up a tree – but I can't tell you what it is 'cause my owner says we can't print it in this family paper). But there are two less of them around here than the last time I wrote about them … 'cause they yelled when they should have run!

Y — Year older now, was 3 on Dec. 5. My two new hunting friends gave me four steaks for my birthday 'cause we've had good luck hunting together. I did share two steaks somewhat with my owner and his wife.

E — Eat, eat and eat … My owner says I have "a cast iron" stomach. I don't know what that means, but maybe it's 'cause I eat dog food, chew bones and biscuits, fish, steak, turkey, chicken breast and vitamins!

A — All of you are special to me this year!

R — Ringneck pheasants, my favorite sport … retrieve them back as I cavort!

Savvy

I've Been In The "Doghouse"

Dog-gone good wishes to all you readers from here on the north shore of Lake Minnewashta. I've been real busy lately and some of my cavortings got me in a little trouble … so I wanted to growl my side of the story.

First off, one of the tricks I learned from my owner was when we come back from our early morning walk, our morning paper is rolled up in our driveway. I've learned to pick it up and take it in the house and give it to Mary or him. One morning not long ago when we got back, my best friend Lucy was out and we roared around while our owners gabbed. I told Lucy about my trick and wanted to show off, so I took the papers from our neighbors Mettlers' and Huses' houses, too! When I tried to take them in to our house was when I got in the doghouse!

Then last Friday, I got my spring trim from Kelly at Doggie Motel and went right up to our vets for my yearly physical. I got so many vaccinations I thought I was a pin cushion! So we get home, all clean, and my owner gives me some chew stuff to clean my teeth. Then we go for a workout in the fields, all smelling and looking good! Can I help it I found some tasty deer poop to eat? After raising his voice (I can tell he's upset with me when that happens), he yelled, "Aack!" (Whatever that means). I just told him I was only doing what came naturally at that canine moment!

I have been having a lot of fun lately 'cause all the snow has melted so we've been doing much running and walking. (I run, he walks!) We've been in some acres where we hunted last fall. My owner told me the best news is that I haven't found any dead pheasants who might have gotten caught in all those heavy snows in December when we quit hunting. I have met some live ones, though! I told them I would be back to visit them in late October.

Speaking of pheasants, I've been "hounding" my owner to take me to the Pheasants Forever Banquet Saturday night, but he won't! He said there would be over 600 there! Can you imagine me with 600 pheasants?? That would be a dream come true! Then he said there may be a lab pup there. I told him my best friend Lucy is a lab, so why can't I go? Maybe he'll change his mind. I told him I'd be on my best behavior and sit and watch … and eat prime rib … Hope I can!

I'll take pen in paw and write soon.

Springingly yours,

Savvy

Maybe I'm Barking Up The Wrong Tree!

There's one lucky squirrel (rodent) that just made it up this tree before getting the pleasure of meeting me face to face. My best friend Lucy (the Chocolate Lab who owns the Walkers across the street) and I were visiting last week after one of our neighborhood romps about things that really irritated us. Made us so mad in fact, that we wanted to go and bark up the nearest tree!

First off, there are cats. Now I know that you're thinking we don't like the average household kitty … but we don't mind them at all! In fact, right across the street there is a big cat named Raider, and the three of us get along pretty well. We just ig-nore each other. The cats we come in contact with that really bother us are those two-toned kitties with fluid drive that live in the country. We call them skunks or stinkers. Both Lucy and I have had several run ins with them while we were hunting and we can't figure out why any animal was created with a built-in stinky smell that wants to share it with all dogs!

Lucy and I are also upset that this summer was not as good for fishing in our neigh-borhood as it has been. I don't know if the denizens of the deep in Minnewashta weren't as hungry as they usually are; or if those fishing for them weren't as skilled as usual. Why should I, a Golden Retriever, care about this, you ask? Because … the more fish caught, the better chance that a few may get left on the beach, or in any area around the lake. And then the sun and time makes them just prefect to roll around on and to have their beautiful odor transferred to our coats … Uhmmm, good and squishy!

As my owner and I wrote this column, he scratched my head and said, "Savvy Dog, if you don't like the smell skunks leave on you … how come you roll on dead fish, and end up with a stink almost as bad as the black and white cats give you?"

I rolled my brown eyes at him, stuck my tongue out, and growled, "You humans will never understand … The skunks do it to us without our choice … we choose to roll in a dead fish and smell that way! It's a canine caper!

Smellingly yours,

Savvy

I Had A Grrreat 4th …
The Grrrandkids Were Here!

Canine connotations from the north shore of Lake Minnewashta to all you dog owners, canines, and readers … (that should be about everyone). This Golden Retriever had one of her happiest weekends ever! All six grandkids were home, and we had a blast! (No fireworks intended).

Look at the grandkids jumping off the dock! Sometimes I'd wait until they hit the water … then I'd bomb in after them!

It was great fun, but one time it got scary! I told you last time I wrote about those geese that are trying to mess up our neighborhood lawns … Well, Friday, they came back and swam by our dock when we were swimming. Eli and Shaelyn jumped in,

 I followed and then I started swimming after the geese. I got out on our lake and I had chased one bad one who was hissing goose profanity at me.

My owner got worried that I might not get back 'cause I swam so far, so he came out in the boat and pulled me out. I was dog tired! Our neighbors told me they thought I swam halfway across our lake. I don't think I'll do that again! And the goose got away on top of it!

57

We Went Hot Tubbing ...

When the grandkids got done swimming, they'd get in the hot tub. This looked like a lot of fun, so I climbed the steps and was getting ready to join the crew, when my owner told me that dogs shouldn't go hot tubbing!

We Watched The Fireworks ...

I saw my first July 4th fireworks! Shaelyn, Tyler, my owner and I walked down the bike trail to the bench by the bridge over Lower Gar and Minnewashta and had a perfect view out over the lake. The fireworks were pretty, but they reminded me of pheasant season opener! A lot of noise (shooting) and as each went through the sky, it looked like the pretty birds flying away after my owner and his hunting friends missed them ...

So, thanks to Shaelyn, Eli, Olivia, Tyler, Isaac and Mya ... They helped make my weekend golden.

See you soon ...

Savvy

I Go To A Party!

In my doggie diatribe of last week, you saw that I got invited to a special benefit party Sunday afternoon. It was put on by the nice people at People for Pets and held at The Chateau on West Okoboji.

I knew it was going to be a special party 'cause I had to take a bath before I went! I think my owner is learning, half the shampoo, half the water, half the time = a happier me! We arrived right after 4:00 PM and I was so excited 'cause I was going to finally get to meet Abby and Grace, the Golden Retrievers who live there! The party was fun, the only thing I was sad about was that Abby was sick (I think she ate too many appetizers before the party) and Grace is a little shy around a crowd.

But I had a toot! The picture above shows me with my owner and two of the neat humans who helped set up the party, Dorothy and Meghan. When we got there, Meghan took my owner on a tour of The Chateau and two nice volunteers walked me around the grounds while I met some of the guests. People told me they read my column and that made me smile!

When he came back to get me on my walk, I got to check out the appetizer table. But I couldn't eat any! I was mad and growled "why." We went for a little walk and he told me there are certain kinds of appetizers human eat … and that my appetizers that I get a lot are just as good … like dog bones, cheese pieces, and fish.

I learned that People for Pets helps pets (that aren't as lucky as me and don't have a good home) to find a good home! They get adopted by loving humans and that's dog-gone ggrrreat news! It was sure a fun party and as I was leaving, Grace and Abby's owners invited me back for a swimming party next week! I'll get to do my "high dive bomb in" off their dock.

Hope you have a grreat week, and that your parties are fun!

Savvy

A Great Weekend of Pheasant Hunting

Boy, did I ever have fun this past weekend! I got to do a lot of what I love doing the most (besides eating and sleeping) and that's hunting for pheasants.

Saturday, I finally got to go hunting with my best friend, Lucy, the Chocolate Lab who owns the Walkers across the street. Both our owners hunt a lot, but they never let us go together. I think they were worried that because we play so hard together we'd mess around and wouldn't hunt well. So Lucy and I got in the back of the van going to the fields, and growled it over. We decided that we'd divide the CRP patch up, hunt our side and meet in the middle. It worked great and our owners were so proud of us! The only thing that didn't go well was that we flushed up all hens except one.

This is an irritant to me! A pheasant smells like a pheasant to a hunting dog! So when we work hard, nose to the ground and get the bird to fly, and no one shoots at it, it drives us barkingly bonkers! By the way, Lucy got up a rooster and I found out her owner shoots like my owner! I think the bird is still flying … but we loved working together!

Sunday, I got to meet two of my owner's friends from Spirit Lake, Steve and John. Steve is an "old" hunting friend, I guess they hunted together 20 years ago. I didn't mean old, 'cause I haven't met many of my owners friends who are older than he is!

We hunted west and south of Milford on some land Steve knows. That was a blast! There was this strip of land, weed patch, and it had birds in it. I think I did OK, flushed up four roosters, (they got three and my owner actually got in on one); and also got up five hens. The fun thing about hunting besides the flushing is retrieving, and its especially a toot to outsmart a rooster who is trying to outsmart me! It was really windy … the one rooster that was missed I think ended up down by Spencer.

Steve and John said they had a real good time with me and asked me to got out next week with them … Funny thing, I don't think they asked my owner!

Well, it was fun visiting with you all, I've got to take a "dog nap" now, (no felines in this column) … all this hunting tires me out … but what a grrreat feeling.

Have a nice Thanksgiving and remember to give your favorite canine a little turkey.

Dreaming … of a rooster.

Savvy

Doggone It ... This Snow Has Got To Go!

I know what you are thinking as you start to read this canine's conversation. "Hey,
dogs are supposed to like snow." Yes, when
I first saw it late this fall, and even pheasant
hunting in it 'til mid-December was fun. But
enough is enough! This snow has cramped
my style, and I'm sure yours, too (although
I can probably get around better on my four
legs than you can on your two.)

It's tough going for this Golden Retriever! Just
look at the picture of me beside a big moun-
tain of snow on my nature trail daily run. I try
to branch out and go where I went this fall, in
the woods and through the slough. But, I end
up getting stuck or even spinning my legs in
snow up past my tummy!

The only good thing about this snow is that
the stinkers (skunks) are sleeping. On one
of our last pheasant hunts in December, my
friend John T. told me that skunks "hibernate" and I wouldn't have any more run ins
like the time I got smelly from the stinkers in November. I don't know what hibernate
means, but I think it is that skunks get tired of smelling bad ... so they try to sleep off
the stink!

One creature I do feel sorry for is the pheasant. Now I know, you're going to say,
"How can that be, Savvy, you're always talking about all the fun it is to hunt them."
Well, I want a fair game ... Right now, even if I could hunt them I wouldn't, 'cause
they're having such a tough time finding food. They're not lucky like me, with great
food and treats everyday! I hope they all find corn and feel good. Then we can start
being adversaries again next fall!

On that same day I fell in the snow bank, I also ran into an old friend! Her name is
Boji. We met as she was walking her owner (like me) down by the bridge between
Lower Gar and Minnewashta. She was asking me why I didn't have a sweater on and
boots on my feet like she did! I answered that with my furry coat and "hunting toes" I
didn't need them. We had a great time in the snow!

That's about it from Oak Street... stay warm ... even if you don't have a furry coat ...
and be careful, two legs are harder to walk on than four!

Savvy

My Point of View by Savvy Adams

"Dogging It" During The Holidays
With My Friends ...

Merry Christmas to all you canines and canine owners out there! As a Golden Retriever, I don't really understand what Merry Christmas
means ... but I've heard it a lot ... and this past week, I
learned some more things!

Thursday, I went to a holiday dinner. My owner took me
to Spirit Lake to visit two special friends of his, Dale
and Sarah Lundstrom. I love going there 'cause I get
good treats! This time, I got a chicken breast (no bone)
and four of Sarah's cookies. Then they talked about the
"old days" (that was before me).

Another reason I love going there is 'cause I get to run
around the yard ... and I go into the former dog kennels
on the grounds. As I wrote you before, they used to own Lundstrom Kennels and
Lundstrom Furniture. Many, many, many Golden Retriever puppies and their parents
lived there. As I sniff around those kennels ... I can barkingly tell you I sense the spirit
of many of those Goldens still there ... I just know it!

As we drove home, I barked at him as to what this visit had to do with Christmas?
He told me a big part of Christmas is to remember special people and events that are
a part of your heart. He told me I had a heart and that I'll remember special dogs and
people who have been friends to me ... He told me Dale and Sara were some of the
first businesses to advertise and support this paper that started 36 years ago, and that
loyalty is a special part of our heart. All dogs know what loyalty is ... we build our
lives around it!

I've become good friends lately with Steve Schmidt and John Tonsfeldt, who hunt
with my owner. This pheasant season has been grrreat! I've gotten a lot of work flushing and retrieving. It's nice to have them along, when I flush a rooster ... John usually always hits it ... Steve sometimes hits it ... and my owner hits it weakly (or is it
weekly?) It's especially fun to find the pheasant when they think they can hide and
fool me ... But they don't ... 'cause my nose knows!

Life is grrreat! I hope you all remember your friends and have a
howling happy holiday season.

Savvy

Doggone It ... Summer's About Over ...
But Hunting Season's Almost Here!

Hello to all you canines, canine owners, and readers! This Golden Retriever is a little sad that summer is ending, but I've got a lot of news to share with you. Pheasant hunt-

ing will soon be starting! I've been practicing my retrieves and finding pheasants. Actually, my owner puts this stinky stuff that smells just like a pheasant on our retrieving dummy, and then hides it. I then scent it out (like the picture), and bring it back!

I've been having so much fun fishing! It's so much different from hunting, 'cause I don't get to use my nose ... but I do use my mouth! Almost every night, my owner and his friend Marv cast off our dock. They've been catching Bluegills and Yellow Bass, and I've "caught" four! Actually, they caught them and were taking the fish off the hook to put in their baskets when the Yellow Bass jumped out of their hands and fell to the dock. I "retrieved" them before they got back in the lake!

I'm going to try to read a book! Well, not quite ... but my owner told me all about a wonderful book he's going to buy and read to me. He heard about a book about dogs having a "soul". My owner told me that he thinks dogs have souls. I didn't know what he meant. I thought "souls" were what I used to chew on his shoes when I was a pup. Then he told me three stories to show me that they do.

One story was about a lady out in her boat recently with her Golden Retriever. She suffered a heart attack and fell overboard, with her life jacket on. When help arrived, she had passed away but the Golden Retriever was swimming beside her, pulling her towards shore.

Back many years ago, before I came to live here (about the time of Goldens Autumn and Brandee), my owner knew a lady who had lost her husband and the family had a wonderful dog who loved his master. After his master died, the dog wouldn't eat he was so sad ... and he passed away, too.

I was beginning to understand about soul when he told me to remember two summers ago when the grandkids were swimming in front of our dock. Olivia had a life jacket on, but started to splash around. I thought she was in trouble so I jumped in, grabbed her by the back of her neck / jacket, and was pulling her towards shore 'til they all told me she was OK.

He told me, "Savvy, this is why dogs do have souls, and why you Goldens have been so special to me over the years." And I thought, "Now I know what these feelings are in my canine heart." And now you know!

**Have a gggrrreat week,
I'll take pen in paw again soon.**

Savvy

My Point Of View
by Savannah Adams

P.S.

(Purely Savvy)

Thank You So Much For Buying My Book!

I hope you enjoyed if half as much as I enjoyed writing it. It was so much fun "booking it."

I learned a bunch of new words that I now have to file in my doggy diatribe. One big word was "deadlines." In my retriever world I thought a deadline was what I drew on pheasants we hunt. I get the scent of one and try to figure out the shortest space between the bird and me... Sort of a deadline to the flush of the bird. But wow, I like my hunting word better than my writing one! Lots of times I had to give up an extra walk or work out so my owner and I could finish putting the book together. He did help me a little bit!

Another word was "copy." Funny thing, I thought this meant when I do a good retrieve or trick, my owner tells me "good girl" and I copy what I just did. But writing copy means we wrote, wrote, and wrote some more so you could have a lot of different stories to read!

One word that was hard for me (in both worlds) was "trim". In my canine world my owner watches my diet (especially during hunting season) so I stay trim and in good shape. Sometimes I eat too much and have to trim down! As "we" compiled this book, we had to trim out some of my columns that I had written so all my Savvy Dog dilemmas would fit into four parts.

Finally, I'd like to thank two special people! The first is Laura Breems. She is a graphic artist for our free newspaper. Laura designed the cover of this book, and "we," the three of us, put the different parts of my book together. The second is Lauri Pederson, also a graphic artist for our paper. Lauri types my weekly column and catalogued all my writings, making it easier for us to draw it together. I think they did GGGREAT! **Bark back to me at savvy@savvythedog.com or visit my website: www.savvythedog.com**

Thanks again for helping my dream become a reality

Savvy

Just a Few Words About The "Author".

Photo "Touch of Love... Savvy and John"
Courtesy © 2010 Photography by Karess - Photographer Karess Knudtson
www.photographybykaress.com

I have been privileged to own six golden retrievers. Savvy encompasses the very best qualities of all her previous "ancestors". She epitomizes, like many good dogs, the very traits - loyalty, innocence, caring, love and compassion that many humans sadly lack. She is an absolute joy to pheasant hunt with, take for a walk or workout, or just be around. She has given me far more than I could ever give her. I am so proud to be her owner and "we" hope you enjoy her book!

- John Adams

www.savvythedog.com